A Little Dose of Daily Laughter

Chuckles & Reminders that with God all things are possible!

Inspired by Faith

A Little Dose of Daily Laughter
ISBN 978-0-9835438-5-5

Published by Product Concept Mfg., Inc.
2175 N. Academy Circle #200, Colorado Springs, CO 80909

All scripture quotations are from the King James version
of the Bible unless otherwise noted.

Scriptures taken from the Holy Bible,
New International Version®, NIV®.
Copyright © 1973, 1978, 1984 by Biblica, Inc.™
Used by permission of Zondervan.
All rights reserved worldwide.
www.zondervan.com

Sayings not having a credit listed are contributed by writers
for Product Concept Mfg., Inc. or in a rare case,
the author is unknown.

Written and Compiled by Patricia Mitchell
in association with Product Concept Mfg., Inc.

A Little Dose of Daily Laughter

God has brought me laughter.
Genesis 21:6 NIV

We all have those days when it's good to be reminded that God is good, He loves us, and He is taking care of us. And that's why, out of the blue, He'll send us something to smile about. May this little book of inspirations help you keep the faith-and a sense of humor-every day.

A thankful
   heart
      is one that's
grace-full
         for all
   its blessings.

When I'm
tempted
to laugh at
someone else,
I just look
into the mirror
and find
all the material
I need.

God's
office hours:
24/7.

Lose weight
instantly!
Put all your
worries
on
Him.

You're
on
His
calendar
today...
and
every
day.

When there's
a long
row to hoe,
remember:
He's still in charge
of the garden.

"Send me!
Send me!"
sounded
so exciting...
until God replied,
"OK, I will."

A dandelion
is a simple weed
or a splendid
flower,
depending on
how you
look at it.

Being a
  Christian
isn't a
    position,
  it's a
process.

If you're
struggling
to keep
an even keel,
let Him take
over the oars
for a while.

Behold,
I stand at
the door,
and knock.

Revelation 3:20

Most of the time,
we pretend
we're not home.

If I want Jesus
   to guide my
   footsteps,
I have to get up
   off the chair
and start walking.

God cares about
the big things,
the small things,
and all things
in your life.

Be
stubborn—
never move
out of
the Way.

When life
lets you down,
God
lifts you up.

If God kept a
family photo
album,
your picture
would
be in it.

Deep-seated
troubles and
long-standing
trials are best
handled in
knee-bending
prayer.

God invites us
   to drop our burden
on Him. And unlike
   the dry cleaning,
   we don't have
      to pick it up
again.

Your Father
  is waiting
for you
  to call.

Harboring
a grudge
is like going
in debt—
the pay-back
on both takes
a lot
out of you.

The Top
Ten List
is not a modern
invention.

There's rarely
a bellhop
at the door of
opportunity,
so it pays to
push it open.

More is
accomplished
by folding
the hands
than by
wringing them.

Sometimes
   avoiding sin
is just
   a matter
      of no-ing.

God calls
 the qualified
and qualifies
 the called...
which sort
of wipes out
 all my excuses.

If life were a
do-it-yourself
project,
God would not
have left
Instructions.

God was my
co-pilot
until I realized
I'd better
let Him do
the driving.

Avoid truth
decay—
brush up on
the Bible daily.

Directions
from here to
heaven
can be found in
Genesis
through
Revelation.

Dr. God
has a prescription
for stress—
it's called
prayer.

The problem
I thought
too light to put
in God's hands
became a problem
too heavy for my
shoulders.

PLAN AHEAD!
There wasn't
a cloud in the sky
when Noah
started
building the ark.

Never provide
a harbor
for contempt—
when you least
expect it,
it sails out in
your words
and actions.

People who
accomplish
things that count
are usually
too busy to
count their
accomplishments.

When you
    don't know
    which way
        to turn,
    check the Map.

The quickest way
to become a leader
is to put
everyone else
ahead of yourself.

Count yourself
  blessed
every day,
and you will find
  yourself living
in a world of
  blessings.

Each morning,
God gives us
a rose.
And some of us
will spend the day
complaining
about
the thorns.

Faith is
heaven-sent,
but its maintenance
takes place
on earth.

God places friends
in our path to bring
light to our lives.

Want to know
your priorities?
Look at your
checkbook
and your calendar.

Friendship
ties
two hearts
together.

"Show me your
ways, Lord,
teach me
your paths..."

Ps 25:4 NIV

(...and then help
me get out
of your way!)

God
loves
to get
knee mail.

Don't opt for
fast food
when God
is serving
soul food.

Laughter is
like a blessing
that tickles
from the
inside out.

Thank God
     for little blessings!

Get your
exercise today!
Walk with
the Lord.

When worry is
knocking at
the door,

Let FAITH answer.

Thank You for
all the
good things
You've sent to me
today…
and for all
the bad things
You've kept away.

God is
everywhere...
even at your
wit's end.

Don't tell God
how big the
storm is.
Tell the storm
how big
your God is.

I make more
progress when my
feet are walking
than
when my
mouth is
running.

Gracious...
is what He is.
Goodness...
is in all He does.
Gracious Goodness...
Aren't you glad
to know Him?!

"Before I formed
   thee in the belly
I knew thee..."

Jeremiah 1:5

Dear God...
   Wow!

God doesn't
always choose
to flatten
the mountain...
but He has
promised to
help you
climb it.

Ask for His gifts,
but trust Him
to send you
the right size
and color.

Remember...
there's nothing
too big
(or too small)
to take to
the LORD.

Let's celebrate
today simply
because it's
the day
which the
LORD
hath made!

Psalm 118:24

Jesus gives us
spiritual wealth
so we can go on a
spending spree.

If you
find it hard
to make
a joyful noise
today,

talk to the
Song Leader.

When there's
too much
bad news,
catch up on the
Good News.

I thank God
for those who
know me so well,
and still love
me so much.

Discipleship
requires
on-the-job
training.

Lord, make me
a "lily of
the field".
Help me to grow
without the
"toil and spin"
cycle.

Consider the lilies of the field,
how they grow; they toil not,
neither do they spin.
Matthew 6:28

Forgiveness
pardons
the offender
and frees
the offended.

A kind deed
is a prayer
with two hands
attached.

Some people
set out
to serve God,
but forget
to inform
their hands
and feet.

An understanding
word is like
a salve
for the
hurting soul.

Friends are the
shock absorbers
in the
SUV of life.

Remembering
our roots
keeps us
down
to
earth.

Even if things
start going
wrong,
keep going
right.

Take a lesson
from the
woodpecker:
Use your head!

The Lord
promises
to shower us
with blessings…
but sometimes
we have to
be willing to
step out
in the rain
to catch them.

Remember your Fruit!
At least 5
servings a day!

"...the fruit of the spirit is
love, joy, peace,
longsuffering, kindness,
goodness, faithfulness,
gentleness and self-control."

Galatians 5:22-23

God has made
this day—
but it's up to
you what to
make
of this day.

More
miracles
grow at our
feet
than drop
from
heaven.

Jesus fed 5,000
   people on five
barley loaves
   and two
      small fish.
So why do I
have trouble
   feeding one
little family
on five bags
   of groceries?

We're called
to salt the earth
with God's love,
but some would
rather pepper
the world
with criticism.

If you're
headed in the
wrong direction
on the highway
of life,
God allows
U-turns.

There's no
such thing
    as an "ordinary" day
to those who
    give it that
    something "extra."

God still
works
miracles.

Some
people,
like angels,
leave a hint
of heaven
wherever
they go.

God wants to be
a part of every
little bitty
teeny tiny
itsy bitsy
thing in
your day.

Some people
get frustrated
because they
can't do
everything...
so they end up
doing nothing.

PRAYER–
Your direct
line to God.

Sometimes
miracles
fall from
heaven...
but most
of the time,
they're right
at our feet.

Q: What's the
    recommended
    vitamin for
Christians?

A: B1

Whatever comes
from the heart
quietly touches
every other heart.

Jesus comes
 with a Lifetime
guarantee.

Do the math:

1 cross
+
3 nails
=
4 given

When I get
in a jam,
it's usually
because
I've been picking
forbidden
fruit.

A lot of people
claim they speak
for Jesus,
but I'd rather open
the Bible and
let Him
speak for Himself.

When we don't
see every day
with the eyes
of faith,
we're blind to
everyday
miracles.

Jesus is the
reason for the...
well..
for everything!

When we
start
kneeling down,
things start
looking
up.

Why is it
exhausting
to sit in church
for one hour,
but exhilarating
to sit in front
of the TV
for three?

God...

You Rock!

Psalm 62:2

RELAX...
   God's taking care
of everything.

Life is like
a cup of coffee:
Sometimes
you have
to go through
the grind,
but God fills
it up
with a
special blend.

"You cannot change
the truth,
but the truth
can change you."

-Unknown

God gives us
special people
to keep us
together
when the
rest of life
seems to be
unraveling.

Lighten up!
Let God
carry
your
load.

How will it
 all turn out?
God only knows.
 And thank
 God He does.

Life's challenges
are God's way
of teaching
us to trust Him.

Good friends
are just one
of the little
blessings God
gives us to
bring us joy.

Snuggle down...
    in all the love
and comfort
    God has for you.

Gather
the blessings
of the day.

Life teaches
us to be
more gentle
with ourselves
and others.

When things
are getting
you down,
keep looking up!

Never be too busy...
to be THANKFUL!

God is where the
love is.

In our likenesses,
God gives us joy—
In our differences,
He helps us grow.

Whenever you
feel stuck-
reach up...
and God
will pull
you through.

Sow seeds of kindness-
and you will have
a perpetual harvest.

God is the
Author of life...
and like any
author,
he receives
rejection
notices.

Friends warm
the heart,
lift the spirit,
and bless
your life.

God took the
time to create
the world–
How can we
be too busy
to appreciate it?

Friends are the
closest thing to
angels this side
of heaven.

Think
positively...
Act
purposefully...
Pray
faithfully.

A gentle spirit
    can change the world.

People may
  forget what
you said...
  and they may
forget what
    you did...
but they'll never
ever forget
    the way you
    made them feel.

God knows
every worry
on your mind.
May He give you
peace in your heart.

God hears
every prayer–
even when
it's just a
whisper
of the heart.

Some people
bring light into
the world just
by being in it.

Even in our messes...
God blesses.

Aaaaahhh!
Life is good.
Give thanks.

At unexpected
moments
God places
an angel
in your path...
someone you
may soon call "friend".

Sometimes you
  find your very
best friend
  is right in your
own family.

Faith is the bridge
between
HOPING and
KNOWING
God is with us.

God has
a special
PURPOSE
just for you.

Every day...
God gives us
a chance to
make a
DIFFERENCE.

Kindness
costs nothing–
but it's the
most precious
gift you can
give someone.

A good memory
can remember
the day's blessings
and forget the
day's troubles.

God can
handle the
    big things...
and all those
little things
    that drive you
        bananas, too.

Sorrow looks back.
Worry looks around.
Faith looks up.

Listen–
   and you'll
   hear an angel
whispering
   "God's taking
      care of
   everything."